ALL AROUND THE WORLD
ISRAEL

by Kristine Spanier

pogo

Ideas for Parents and Teachers

Pogo Books let children practice reading informational text while introducing them to nonfiction features such as headings, labels, sidebars, maps, and diagrams, as well as a table of contents, glossary, and index.

Carefully leveled text with a strong photo match offers early fluent readers the support they need to succeed.

Before Reading

- "Walk" through the book and point out the various nonfiction features. Ask the student what purpose each feature serves.
- Look at the glossary together. Read and discuss the words.

Read the Book

- Have the child read the book independently.
- Invite him or her to list questions that arise from reading.

After Reading

- Discuss the child's questions. Talk about how he or she might find answers to those questions.
- Prompt the child to think more. Ask: What did you know about Israel before you read this book? What more would you like to learn?

Pogo Books are published by Jump!
5357 Penn Avenue South
Minneapolis, MN 55419
www.jumplibrary.com

Library of Congress Cataloging-in-Publication Data

Names: Spanier, Kristine, author.
Title: Israel / by Kristine Spanier.
Description: Minneapolis, MN : Pogo Books, 2020.
Series: All around the world | Includes bibliographical references and index. | Audience: 7-10.
Identifiers: LCCN 2018044421 (print)
LCCN 2018046271 (ebook)
ISBN 9781641286497 (e-book)
ISBN 9781641286473 (hardcover : alk. paper)
ISBN 9781641286480 (pbk.)
Subjects: LCSH: Israel—Juvenile literature.
Classification: LCC DS118 (ebook)
LCC DS118 .S653 2020 (print) | DDC 956.94—dc23
LC record available at https://lccn.loc.gov/2018044421

Editor: Susanne Bushman
Designer: Molly Ballanger

Photo Credits: Chr. Offenberg/Shutterstock, cover; etorres/Shutterstock, 1; Pixfiction/Shutterstock, 3; VanderWolf Images/Shutterstock, 4; michelangeloop/Shutterstock, 5; Jose Marie Hernandez/123rf, 6-7; By-Taurus-/Shutterstock, 8-9; wavemovies/iStock, 10; Simon Dawson/Bloomberg/Getty, 11; Seth Aronstam/Shutterstock, 12-13; AHMAD GHARABLI/AFP/Getty, 14-15; lom66/iStock, 16, 20-21b; Oleg Zaslavsky/Shutterstock, 17; RuslanDashinsky/iStock, 18-19; tony mills/Shutterstock, 20t; Toovit Begun Photography/Shutterstock, 20b; Wildlife World/Shutterstock, 20-21t; The World in HDR/Shutterstock, 23.

Printed in the United States of America at Corporate Graphics in North Mankato, Minnesota.

TABLE OF CONTENTS

CHAPTER 1

WELCOME TO ISRAEL!

Visit the Dome of the Rock. It is a holy place. For who? Jewish and Muslim people. It was built in the 690s!

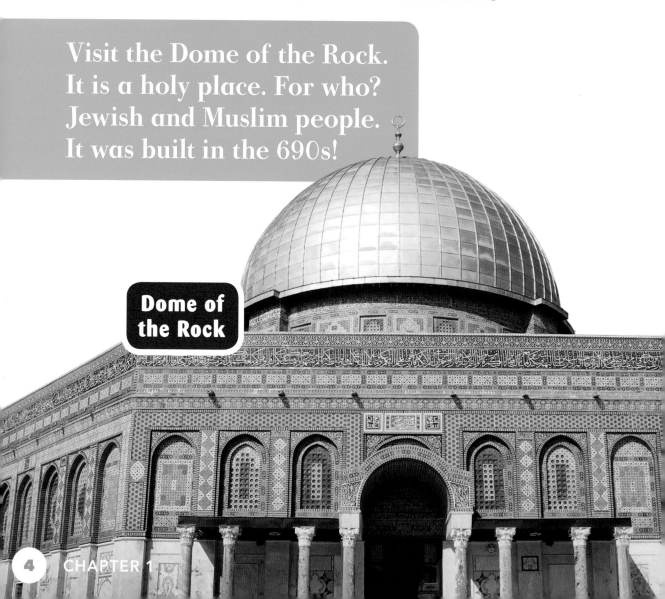

Dome of the Rock

See the **ruins** of King Herod's palace. He became king in 37 BCE. You are in Israel!

Israel formed in 1948. Why? To be a homeland for Jewish people. Arabs live here, too. They are called Palestinians. Many of them do not want Israel to be a Jewish country.

This conflict caused two wars. One was in 1967. This was the Six-Day War. The Yom Kippur War was in 1973. There is still conflict here today.

DID YOU KNOW?

Israel has a strong **military**. All non-Palestinian men and women must join. When? At the age of 18. They serve two to three years.

prayers · · · · · · ·

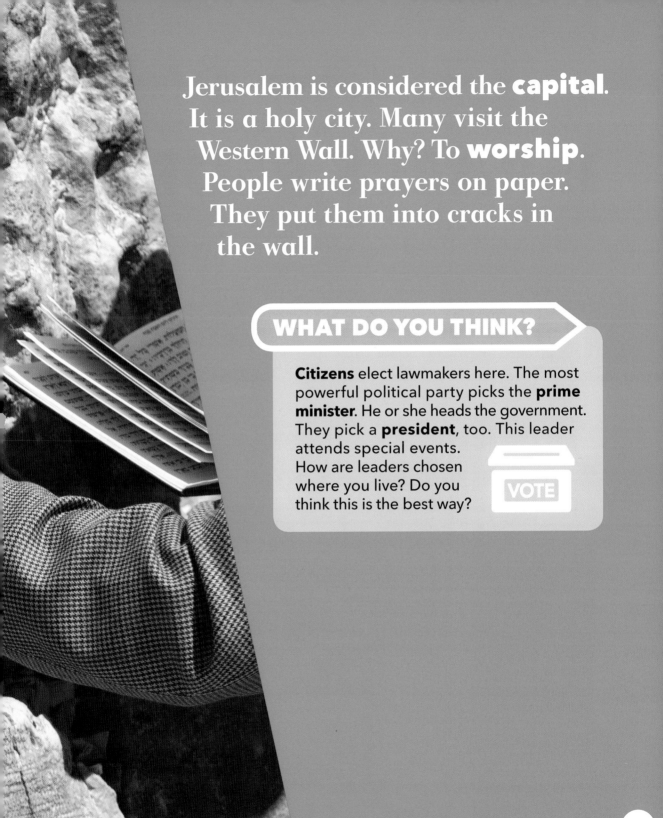

Jerusalem is considered the **capital**. It is a holy city. Many visit the Western Wall. Why? To **worship**. People write prayers on paper. They put them into cracks in the wall.

WHAT DO YOU THINK?

Citizens elect lawmakers here. The most powerful political party picks the **prime minister**. He or she heads the government. They pick a **president**, too. This leader attends special events. How are leaders chosen where you live? Do you think this is the best way?

VOTE

CHAPTER 2

ISRAEL'S PEOPLE

Most Israelis live in cities. They live in small apartments. They take trains or buses to get around. Bicycles are popular in Tel Aviv. This is the country's second largest city.

Tel Aviv

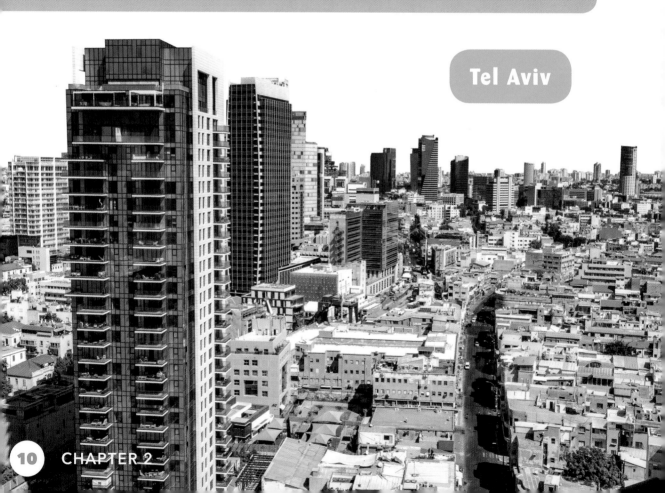

diamond

Many people work developing technology. Like what? Jets. Medical equipment. Cell phones. Some work cutting and polishing diamonds. Many have jobs in **tourism**.

Jewish people from around the world can become citizens here. This is called the Law of Return. Many **immigrate** here. From where? Europe. Other parts of the Middle East, too.

TAKE A LOOK!

Jewish people make up a **majority** of the **population** here. Arabs are the largest **minority**.

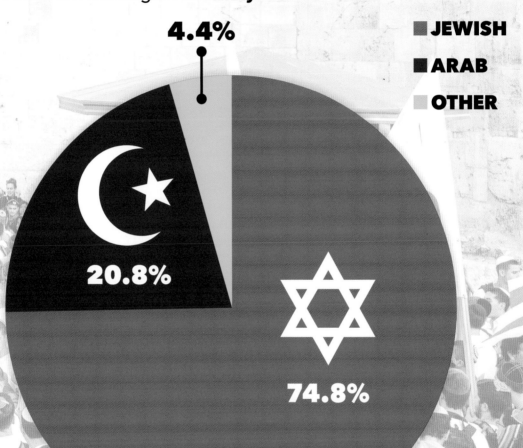

4.4%

20.8%

74.8%

■ JEWISH
■ ARAB
■ OTHER

Children wear uniforms to school. They learn different languages. Which ones? English. Arabic. Hebrew. Students go to school six days a week. They have Saturdays off. This is a day for rest and worship.

WHAT DO YOU THINK?

Jewish and Arab students go to separate schools. Do you think they should attend the same schools? Why or why not?

CHAPTER 3

LAND AND ANIMALS

Coastal **plains** lie along the Mediterranean Sea. The Negev is a desert region in the south.

Negev

Good farmland is in the east.
What **crops** grow here?
Citrus fruits. Olives. Dates.
Grapes. Vegetables.

dates

The Dead Sea is in the east.
It is the lowest place on Earth.
It is below sea level. How far?
More than 1,400 feet (427 meters).
It is very salty. Fish and plants
cannot live in it. But people
enjoy floating in it!

warbler

cuckoo

lupine

papyrus reeds

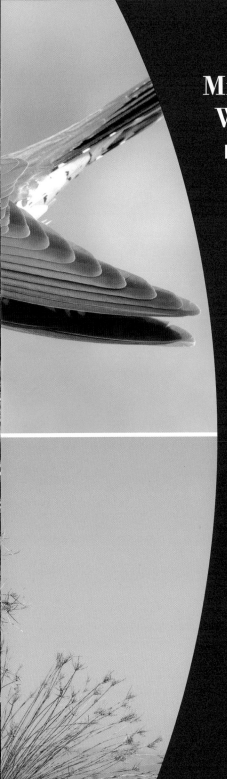

Millions of birds fly over Israel. When? During their yearly **migrations**. Hula Valley is one place to see this. Here you will find partridges. Warblers. Cuckoos. Desert larks.

Israel has many kinds of plants. How many? More than 2,800! Like what? Coral peonies. Lupine. Desert papyrus reeds. Pretty!

This is a fascinating country. Would you like to visit?

QUICK FACTS & TOOLS

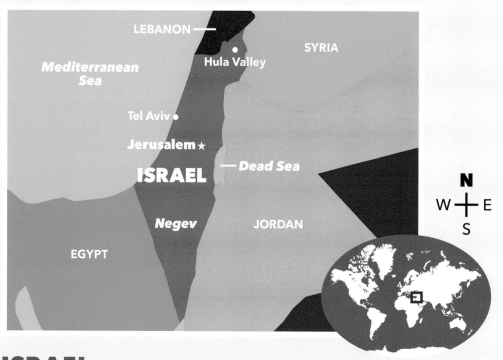

ISRAEL

Location: Middle East

Size: 8,019 square miles (20,770 square kilometers)

Population: 8,424,904 (July 2018 estimate)

Capital: Jerusalem

Type of Government: parliamentary democracy

Languages: Hebrew and Arabic

Exports: machinery, software, diamonds, agricultural products

Currency: Israeli new shekel

GLOSSARY

capital: A city where government leaders meet.

citizens: People who have full rights in a certain country, such as the right to work and the right to vote.

crops: Plants grown for food.

immigrate: To move from one country to another and settle there.

majority: More than half of the people in a group.

migrations: Movements of people or animals from one region or habitat to another.

military: The armed forces in a country.

minority: Less than half of the people in a group.

plains: Large, flat areas of land.

population: The total number of people who live in a place.

president: A leader of a country, sometimes in a ceremonial position.

prime minister: The leader of a country.

ruins: The remains of something that has collapsed or been destroyed.

tourism: The business of serving people who are traveling for pleasure.

worship: To show love and devotion to God or a god, especially by praying or going to a church service.

Israel's currency

INDEX

TO LEARN MORE

Finding more information is as easy as 1, 2, 3.

1. Go to www.factsurfer.com

2. Enter "Israel" into the search box.

3. Click the "Surf" button to see a list of websites.

FACT SURFER